THIS PLANNER
belongs to

SCHOOL	ROOM
GRADE	ADDRESS

EMAIL

PHONE

CONTACTS and Volunteers

NAME	CONTACT INFO

WELCOME

SCHEDULE

SCHOOL BEGINS: ______

LUNCH: ______

RECESS: ______

SPECIALS: ______

SCHOOL ENDS: ______

NEED HELP?

RELIABLE STUDENTS: ______

TEACHERS: ______

PRINCIPAL: ______

VICE PRINCIPAL: ______

OTHER STAFF: ______

SPECIAL SCHEDULES

NAMES	TIME | LOCATION

ADDITIONAL NOTES

COMMUNICATION LOG

DATE	TYPE	NAME	PURPOSE	NOTES

COMMUNICATION LOG

DATE	TYPE	NAME	PURPOSE	NOTES
	@			
	@			
	@			
	@			
	@			
	@			
	@			
	@			
	@			
	@			
	@			
	@			
	@			
	@			
	@			
	@			
	@			
	@			
	@			
	@			
	@			
	@			
	@			
	@			
	@			
	@			

NEWS & NOTES

NEWS & NOTES

PLAN IT

USE THESE PAGES TO CREATE A CLASSROOM PLAN, RECORD SEATING CHARTS, CREATE CHECKLISTS, SKETCH PLANS, ETC. THE OPTIONS ARE ENDLESS!

YEAR AT A GLANCE

JULY

AUGUST

SEPTEMBER

OCTOBER

NOVEMBER

DECEMBER

JANUARY
FEBRUARY
MARCH
APRIL
MAY
JUNE

JULY

Be like a tree—stand tall but be flexible.

SUNDAY	MONDAY	TUESDAY	WEDNESDAY

IMPORTANT DATES

GOALS

THURSDAY	FRIDAY	SATURDAY

HAVE TO DO

NOTES

PSST! USE THESE GUIDES TO KEEP YOUR TABS PERFECTLY PLACED.

AUGUST

You can move mountains.

SUNDAY	MONDAY	TUESDAY	WEDNESDAY

IMPORTANT DATES

GOALS

THURSDAY	FRIDAY	SATURDAY

HAVE TO DO

NOTES

SEPTEMBER

Allow room to fail; it makes more space to grow.

SUNDAY	MONDAY	TUESDAY	WEDNESDAY

IMPORTANT DATES

GOALS

THURSDAY	FRIDAY	SATURDAY

HAVE TO DO

NOTES

OCTOBER

Find beauty in the little things.

SUNDAY	MONDAY	TUESDAY	WEDNESDAY

IMPORTANT DATES

GOALS

THURSDAY	FRIDAY	SATURDAY

HAVE TO DO

NOTES

NOVEMBER

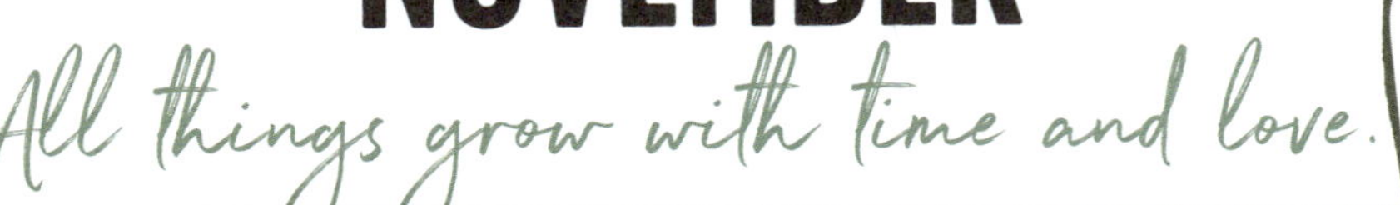

SUNDAY	MONDAY	TUESDAY	WEDNESDAY

IMPORTANT DATES

GOALS

THURSDAY	FRIDAY	SATURDAY

HAVE TO DO

NOTES

DECEMBER

It may not be easy, but it will be worth it.

SUNDAY	MONDAY	TUESDAY	WEDNESDAY

IMPORTANT DATES

GOALS

THURSDAY	FRIDAY	SATURDAY

HAVE TO DO

NOTES

JANUARY

Love grows here.

SUNDAY	MONDAY	TUESDAY	WEDNESDAY

IMPORTANT DATES

GOALS

THURSDAY	FRIDAY	SATURDAY

HAVE TO DO

NOTES

FEBRUARY

Teachers make futures blossom.

SUNDAY	MONDAY	TUESDAY	WEDNESDAY

IMPORTANT DATES

GOALS

THURSDAY	FRIDAY	SATURDAY

HAVE TO DO

NOTES

MARCH

Every day is a fresh start.

SUNDAY	MONDAY	TUESDAY	WEDNESDAY

IMPORTANT DATES

GOALS

THURSDAY	FRIDAY	SATURDAY

HAVE TO DO

NOTES

APRIL

Slow down and enjoy each moment.

SUNDAY	MONDAY	TUESDAY	WEDNESDAY

IMPORTANT DATES

GOALS

THURSDAY	FRIDAY	SATURDAY

HAVE TO DO

NOTES

MAY

Give yourself time to grow.

SUNDAY	MONDAY	TUESDAY	WEDNESDAY

IMPORTANT DATES

GOALS

THURSDAY	FRIDAY	SATURDAY

HAVE TO DO

NOTES

JUNE

Grow through what you go through.

SUNDAY	MONDAY	TUESDAY	WEDNESDAY

IMPORTANT DATES

GOALS

THURSDAY	FRIDAY	SATURDAY

HAVE TO DO

NOTES

WEEK #

SUBJECT	SUBJECT	SUBJECT

MONDAY

TUESDAY

WEDNESDAY

THURSDAY

FRIDAY

SUBJECT	SUBJECT	SUBJECT	SUBJECT

PSST! CUT THIS CORNER OFF EACH WEEK TO MARK AND FIND YOUR PLACE EASILY.

WEEK #

	SUBJECT	SUBJECT	SUBJECT
MONDAY			
TUESDAY			
WEDNESDAY			
THURSDAY			
FRIDAY			

SUBJECT	SUBJECT	SUBJECT	SUBJECT

WEEK #

SUBJECT	SUBJECT	SUBJECT

MONDAY

TUESDAY

WEDNESDAY

THURSDAY

FRIDAY

SUBJECT	SUBJECT	SUBJECT	SUBJECT

WEEK #

	SUBJECT	SUBJECT	SUBJECT
MONDAY			
TUESDAY			
WEDNESDAY			
THURSDAY			
FRIDAY			

SUBJECT	SUBJECT	SUBJECT	SUBJECT

WEEK #

	SUBJECT	SUBJECT	SUBJECT
MONDAY			
TUESDAY			
WEDNESDAY			
THURSDAY			
FRIDAY			

SUBJECT	SUBJECT	SUBJECT	SUBJECT

WEEK #

	SUBJECT	SUBJECT	SUBJECT
MONDAY			
TUESDAY			
WEDNESDAY			
THURSDAY			
FRIDAY			

SUBJECT	SUBJECT	SUBJECT	SUBJECT

WEEK #
SUBJECT
SUBJECT
SUBJECT
MONDAY
TUESDAY
WEDNESDAY
THURSDAY
FRIDAY

SUBJECT	SUBJECT	SUBJECT	SUBJECT

WEEK #

SUBJECT	SUBJECT	SUBJECT

MONDAY

TUESDAY

WEDNESDAY

THURSDAY

FRIDAY

SUBJECT	SUBJECT	SUBJECT	SUBJECT

WEEK #

	SUBJECT	SUBJECT	SUBJECT
MONDAY			
TUESDAY			
WEDNESDAY			
THURSDAY			
FRIDAY			

SUBJECT	SUBJECT	SUBJECT	SUBJECT

WEEK #

SUBJECT	SUBJECT	SUBJECT

MONDAY

TUESDAY

WEDNESDAY

THURSDAY

FRIDAY

SUBJECT	SUBJECT	SUBJECT	SUBJECT

WEEK #

SUBJECT	SUBJECT	SUBJECT

MONDAY

TUESDAY

WEDNESDAY

THURSDAY

FRIDAY

SUBJECT	SUBJECT	SUBJECT	SUBJECT

WEEK #

	SUBJECT	SUBJECT	SUBJECT
MONDAY			
TUESDAY			
WEDNESDAY			
THURSDAY			
FRIDAY			

SUBJECT	SUBJECT	SUBJECT	SUBJECT

WEEK #

SUBJECT	SUBJECT	SUBJECT

MONDAY

TUESDAY

WEDNESDAY

THURSDAY

FRIDAY

SUBJECT	SUBJECT	SUBJECT	SUBJECT

WEEK #

	SUBJECT	SUBJECT	SUBJECT
MONDAY			
TUESDAY			
WEDNESDAY			
THURSDAY			
FRIDAY			

SUBJECT	SUBJECT	SUBJECT	SUBJECT

WEEK #

	SUBJECT	SUBJECT	SUBJECT
MONDAY			
TUESDAY			
WEDNESDAY			
THURSDAY			
FRIDAY			

SUBJECT	SUBJECT	SUBJECT	SUBJECT

WEEK #

	SUBJECT	SUBJECT	SUBJECT
MONDAY			
TUESDAY			
WEDNESDAY			
THURSDAY			
FRIDAY			

SUBJECT	SUBJECT	SUBJECT	SUBJECT

WEEK #

SUBJECT	SUBJECT	SUBJECT

MONDAY

TUESDAY

WEDNESDAY

THURSDAY

FRIDAY

SUBJECT	SUBJECT	SUBJECT	SUBJECT

WEEK #

SUBJECT	SUBJECT	SUBJECT

MONDAY

TUESDAY

WEDNESDAY

THURSDAY

FRIDAY

SUBJECT	SUBJECT	SUBJECT	SUBJECT

WEEK #

SUBJECT	SUBJECT	SUBJECT

MONDAY

TUESDAY

WEDNESDAY

THURSDAY

FRIDAY

SUBJECT	SUBJECT	SUBJECT	SUBJECT

WEEK #

SUBJECT	SUBJECT	SUBJECT

MONDAY

TUESDAY

WEDNESDAY

THURSDAY

FRIDAY

SUBJECT
SUBJECT
SUBJECT
SUBJECT

WEEK #

SUBJECT	SUBJECT	SUBJECT

MONDAY

TUESDAY

WEDNESDAY

THURSDAY

FRIDAY

SUBJECT	SUBJECT	SUBJECT	SUBJECT

WEEK #

SUBJECT	SUBJECT	SUBJECT

MONDAY

TUESDAY

WEDNESDAY

THURSDAY

FRIDAY

SUBJECT	SUBJECT	SUBJECT	SUBJECT

WEEK #

	SUBJECT	SUBJECT	SUBJECT
MONDAY			
TUESDAY			
WEDNESDAY			
THURSDAY			
FRIDAY			

SUBJECT	SUBJECT	SUBJECT	SUBJECT

WEEK #

	SUBJECT	SUBJECT	SUBJECT
MONDAY			
TUESDAY			
WEDNESDAY			
THURSDAY			
FRIDAY			

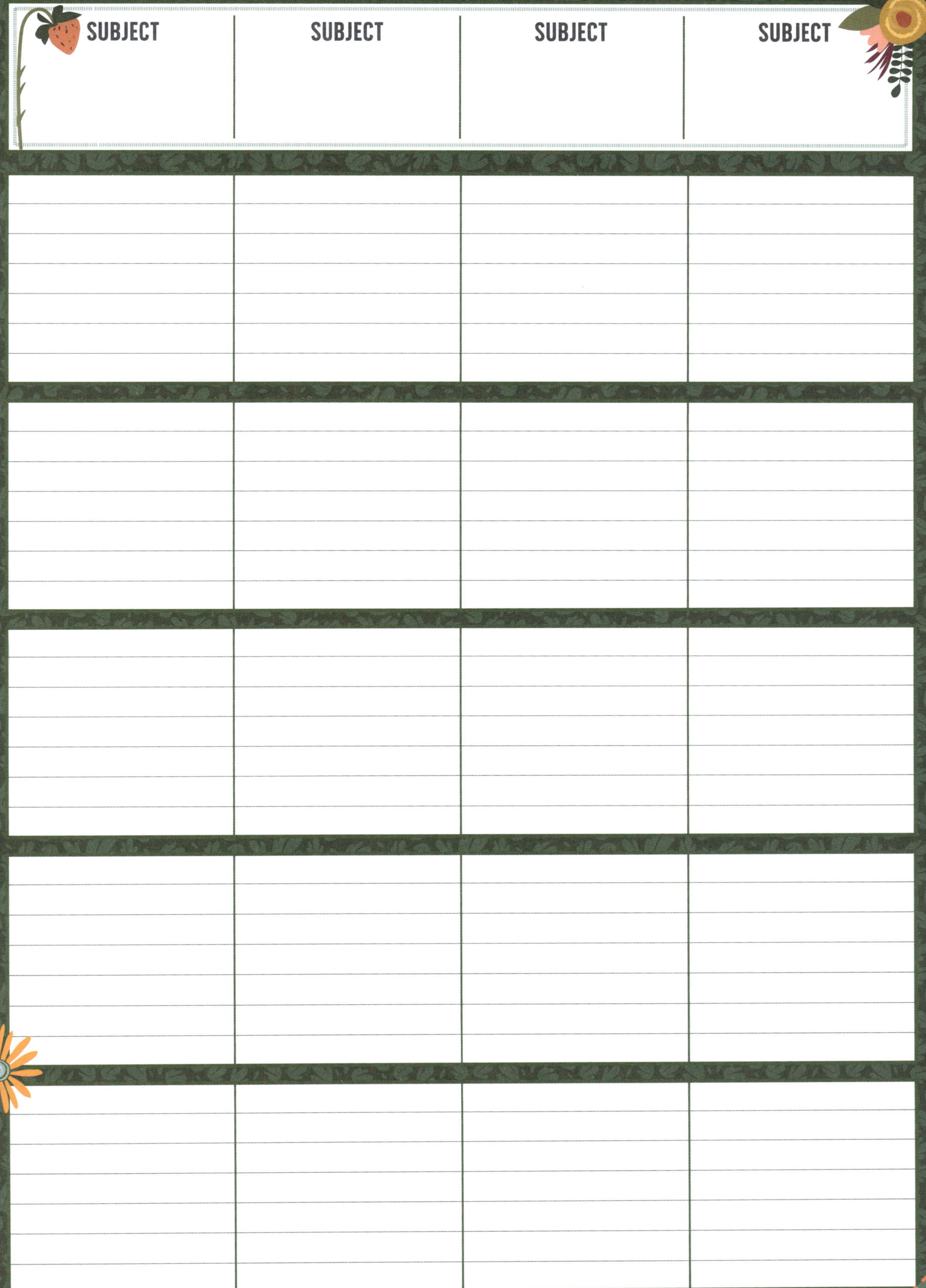

SUBJECT	SUBJECT	SUBJECT	SUBJECT

WEEK #

SUBJECT	SUBJECT	SUBJECT

MONDAY

TUESDAY

WEDNESDAY

THURSDAY

FRIDAY

SUBJECT	SUBJECT	SUBJECT	SUBJECT

WEEK #

	SUBJECT	SUBJECT	SUBJECT
MONDAY			
TUESDAY			
WEDNESDAY			
THURSDAY			
FRIDAY			

SUBJECT	SUBJECT	SUBJECT	SUBJECT

WEEK #

SUBJECT	SUBJECT	SUBJECT

MONDAY

TUESDAY

WEDNESDAY

THURSDAY

FRIDAY

SUBJECT	SUBJECT	SUBJECT	SUBJECT

WEEK #

SUBJECT	SUBJECT	SUBJECT

MONDAY

TUESDAY

WEDNESDAY

THURSDAY

FRIDAY

SUBJECT	SUBJECT	SUBJECT	SUBJECT

WEEK #

SUBJECT	SUBJECT	SUBJECT

MONDAY

TUESDAY

WEDNESDAY

THURSDAY

FRIDAY

SUBJECT	SUBJECT	SUBJECT	SUBJECT

WEEK #

SUBJECT	SUBJECT	SUBJECT

MONDAY

TUESDAY

WEDNESDAY

THURSDAY

FRIDAY

SUBJECT	SUBJECT	SUBJECT	SUBJECT

WEEK #

SUBJECT	SUBJECT	SUBJECT

MONDAY

TUESDAY

WEDNESDAY

THURSDAY

FRIDAY

SUBJECT	SUBJECT	SUBJECT	SUBJECT

WEEK #

SUBJECT	SUBJECT	SUBJECT

MONDAY

TUESDAY

WEDNESDAY

THURSDAY

FRIDAY

SUBJECT	SUBJECT	SUBJECT	SUBJECT

WEEK #

	SUBJECT	SUBJECT	SUBJECT
MONDAY			
TUESDAY			
WEDNESDAY			
THURSDAY			
FRIDAY			

SUBJECT	SUBJECT	SUBJECT	SUBJECT

WEEK #

	SUBJECT	SUBJECT	SUBJECT
MONDAY			
TUESDAY			
WEDNESDAY			
THURSDAY			
FRIDAY			

SUBJECT	SUBJECT	SUBJECT	SUBJECT

WEEK #

SUBJECT	SUBJECT	SUBJECT

MONDAY

TUESDAY

WEDNESDAY

THURSDAY

FRIDAY

SUBJECT	SUBJECT	SUBJECT	SUBJECT

WEEK #

SUBJECT	SUBJECT	SUBJECT

MONDAY

TUESDAY

WEDNESDAY

THURSDAY

FRIDAY

SUBJECT	SUBJECT	SUBJECT	SUBJECT

WEEK #

SUBJECT	SUBJECT	SUBJECT

MONDAY

TUESDAY

WEDNESDAY

THURSDAY

FRIDAY

SUBJECT	SUBJECT	SUBJECT	SUBJECT

WEEK #

SUBJECT	SUBJECT	SUBJECT

MONDAY

TUESDAY

WEDNESDAY

THURSDAY

FRIDAY

SUBJECT	SUBJECT	SUBJECT	SUBJECT

WEEK #

SUBJECT	SUBJECT	SUBJECT

MONDAY

TUESDAY

WEDNESDAY

THURSDAY

FRIDAY

SUBJECT	SUBJECT	SUBJECT	SUBJECT

WEEK #

	SUBJECT	SUBJECT	SUBJECT
MONDAY			
TUESDAY			
WEDNESDAY			
THURSDAY			
FRIDAY			

SUBJECT	SUBJECT	SUBJECT	SUBJECT

CHECKLIST

Name

PSST! CUT THIS SECTION OFF SO YOU ONLY HAVE TO WRITE YOUR CLASS LIST ONCE.

CHECKLIST

Name

CHECKLIST

Name

CHECKLIST
Name

CHECKLIST

Name

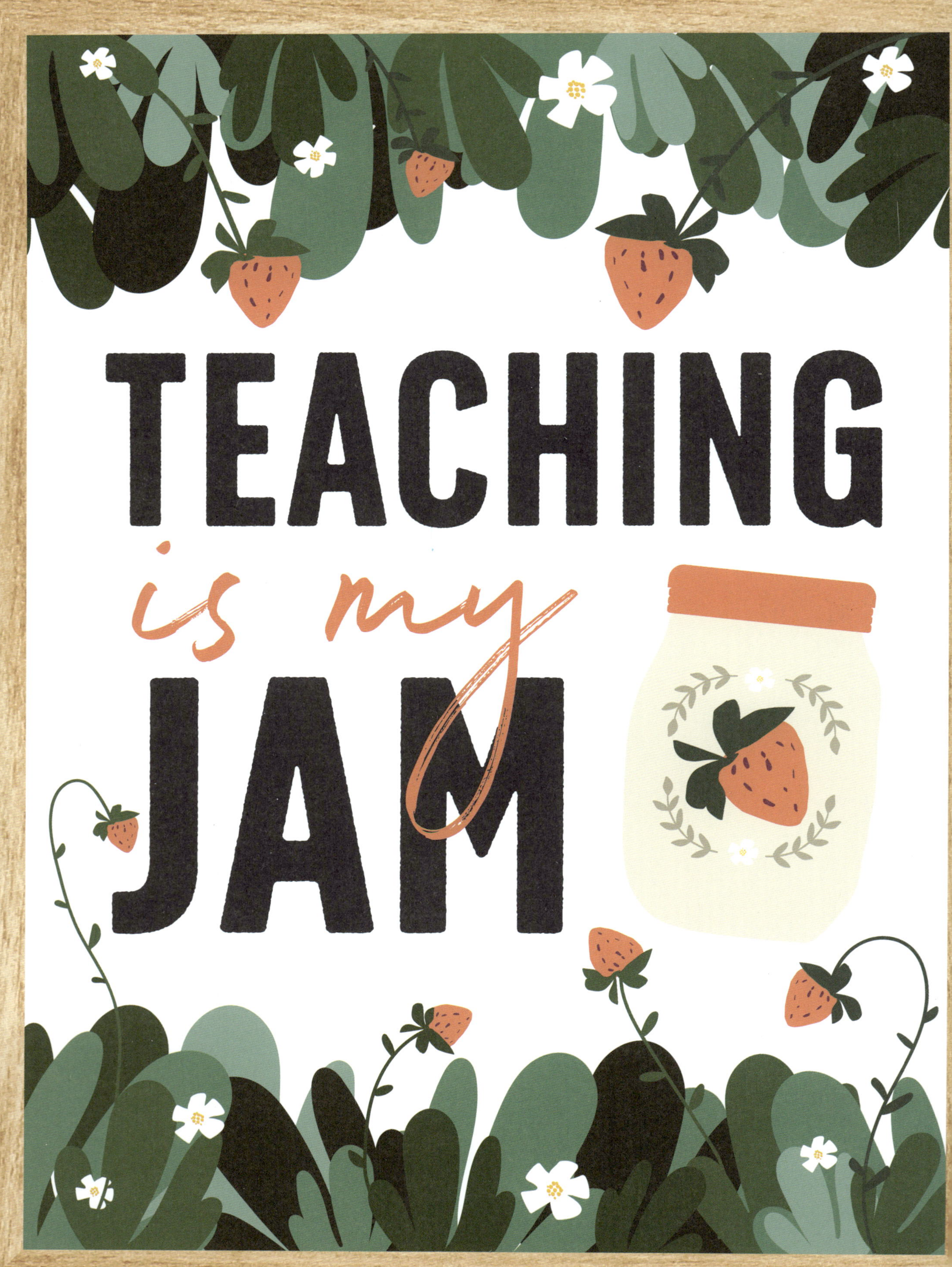
TEACHING
is my
JAM